LEYLAND'S BIG CAT COACHES

HOWARD BERRY

AMBERLEY

First published 2019

Amberley Publishing
The Hill, Stroud
Gloucestershire, GL5 4EP

www.amberley-books.com

Copyright © Howard Berry, 2019

The right of Howard Berry to be identified as
the Author of this work has been asserted in
accordance with the Copyrights, Designs and
Patents Act 1988.

ISBN 978 1 4456 8702 5 (print)
ISBN 978 1 4456 8703 2 (ebook)

British Library Cataloguing in Publication Data.
A catalogue record for this book is available from
the British Library.

Typesetting by Aura Technology and Software
Services, India. Printed in the UK.

Contents

Introduction

Situated some 6 miles south of Preston, the Lancashire town of Leyland could once claim to be home to one of the largest producers of trucks and buses in the world, a company whose humble beginnings were in building steam lawnmowers in a back yard. James Sumner, the son of a blacksmith, inherited his father's business in 1892. Not having an interest in the smithy, he used the premises to indulge in his interest of building steam-powered engines. Expansion followed when George and Henry Spurrier, two brothers from Manchester, acquired a share in the fledgling company, and in 1895 J. Sumner Ltd was formed when Preston-based Coulthard & Co. purchased a half share. A year later the company changed its name to the Lancashire Steam Motor Company and moved to Herbert Street in Leyland, premises large enough to accommodate a workforce by now numbering around twenty. By the end of 1896 the first steam vehicle was produced, and by 1899 passenger-carrying vehicles were being produced. In 1902 a further move was made, this time to Hough Lane in Leyland, as a strong order book and a workforce of 150 meant the company had outgrown the Herbert Street premises.

At the 1905 Commercial Motor Show, the company exhibited a double-decker fitted with a Crossley petrol engine. The company still traded as the Lancashire Steam Motor Co., but the chassis bore the name 'Leyland', and by the end of 1905 six vehicles had been put into service. In 1907 the name was changed to Leyland Motors Ltd and later that year Leyland not only bought out Coulthard's share of the business, but also the company itself. The popularity of petrol-engined vehicles meant that demand for steam vehicles was falling and so steam manufacture was transferred to a smaller factory in nearby Chorley. In 1913 a new site was built at Farington, just north of Leyland, to accommodate the workforce, which now numbered over 1,500.

Leyland was always at the forefront of development and innovation and in 1933 the first Leyland diesel engine for passenger vehicles was exhibited at the Commercial Motor Show. By the end of the year, the diesel engine was available for all models in the Leyland range. Having been interrupted by the war, 1949 saw Leyland return to the development of an underfloor-engined single-deck bus. The advantages of putting the engine under the floor were manifold: increased seating capacity, improved supervision of entry and exit, better weight distribution and improved access to major components, leading to reduced maintenance costs. Joining forces with Metro-Cammell, the Olympic as it was named was not a resounding success but paved the way for the models which were to make Leyland the vehicle manufacturing success it was to become. Leyland was also at the forefront of double-deck bus development, and after overcoming initial difficulties caused by noise levels inside the saloon, the first of the extremely successful Leyland Atlantean model was delivered in 1959.

Acquisitions and mergers saw the formation of the British Leyland Motor Company (BLMC), whose market share had increased to a near monopoly within the UK. The bringing together of companies which had previously been in competition, spread over numerous manufacturing sites and with differing working practices, had taken a toll on the group's finances, and in 1974 the company needed a government guarantee to keep it afloat. The production of cars was an important part of BLMC's business but the financial returns from car production alone were not enough to support the development of new models without support from the commercial vehicle side of the business, leading to a lack of investment in this sector. In order to protect what was one of the UK's major employers, a team led by Lord Ryder recommended splitting BLMC into separate autonomous divisions, one being Leyland Bus & Truck. While there were no recommendations for closures of any plants, the report recommended a massive capital expenditure from the government, and if this advice was not taken it could be construed that the government had allowed the UK's leading vehicle manufacturing company to collapse, leading to around a million people being put out of work. The result of adopting the report was the effective nationalisation of BLMC. In 1981 the Bus & Truck division was split again, with the passenger division being renamed Leyland Bus, and while being given a greater degree of autonomy, its control was still under the auspices of Leyland Vehicles Ltd. This was to remain until January 1987, when Leyland Bus was sold to a consortium formed of senior management and investment banks. By the end of the same year, doubts were raised over the future of the newly privatised company and in March 1988 the company was sold to Volvo. Initially, Leyland Bus operated as a separate division of Volvo, but in September 1988 it was renamed VL Bus & Coach (UK) Ltd, effectively ending over ninety years of the Leyland name.

This, the first in a series of three books looking at the passenger vehicles produced by Leyland, takes a look at Leyland's big cats, the Panther, Leopard, Tiger and Royal Tiger, when used as luxury coaches across the UK. With a starting point of 1960, the story is told through 180 colour photographs with what are (hopefully) informative captions. As with my previous publications, I have been greatly assisted in my endeavours by a handful of photographers to whom I am indebted, not only for letting me use their work, but also for having the foresight to record these vehicles in their heyday for others to enjoy so many years later. Each photographer has an initialled credit after their work, and are Alan Snatt (AS), Cliff Essex (CE), Dave Jones (DJ), John Law (JL), Martyn Hearson (MH), Ray Jones (RJ), Richard Cripps (RC), Richard Simons (RS), Steve Guess (SG), and Terry Walker (TW).

Finally, once again I must say a huge thank you to Sophie (Mrs B) for turning a blind eye to the piles of books I keep leaving on the dining room table, not rolling her eyes in despair (too much) when I tell her I've discovered an interesting fact about a photograph, and saving the day when I again manage to lose track of time and miss the school run.

Howard Berry
Cheswardine, Shropshire

The Leopard

At the Scottish Motor Show in 1959, Leyland unveiled its new medium-weight chassis, the Leopard. Two versions were shown: the L1, with a straight chassis frame and intended primarily for bus work, and the L2, with a stepped rear frame and two-speed axle and more suitable for coach work. Both versions were powered by the 9.8 litre O.600 engine and had a four-speed synchromesh gearbox. The Leopard fitted the gap nicely between the lighter Tiger Cub and the heavy-duty Worldmaster and was essentially a Tiger Cub chassis with a more powerful engine. In 1961, Construction and Use Regulations were amended, bringing Britain into line with most other European countries and allowing the maximum length of a PSV to be increased to 36 feet. It was at that year's Scottish Motor Show that Leyland unveiled its range of longer length Leopards. Offered with synchromesh or pneumocyclic (semi-automatic) gearboxes, the chassis designation was changed to PSU3, and while the L1 and L2 remained available, they were later modified to bring them into line with the PSU3 range, and so were designated PSU4.

From 1966 the Leopard became a true heavyweight chassis when the larger 11.3 litre O.680 engine was made available in vehicles fitted with the pneumocyclic gearbox, and while most operators elected to take the larger engine configuration, the Scottish Bus Group (SBG) continued to take the synchromesh gearbox Leopard with the O.600 engine until it was discontinued in 1973. Construction and Use Regulations were relaxed again in 1967, this time allowing vehicles to be built to a maximum length of 39 feet, and in 1970 the PSU5 was introduced, only available with the pneumocyclic gearbox (which now also included a ten-speed splitter version). It was not until the end of AEC Reliance production in 1979 that the PSU5 was available with a manual gearbox, when pressure from operators loyal to the Reliance persuaded Leyland to introduce a ZF gearbox option to the PSU3 and PSU5.

Throughout its lifespan, the Leopard was subjected to Leyland's programme of continuous improvement, particularly in relation to driver and vehicle safety, and many improvements and alterations to the Leopard chassis were made, mostly in connection to the braking system. In 1982, with the TL11-powered Tiger already launched, the Leopard received a rationalised version of the O.680 which shared numerous TL11 components. Despite these improvements, new European legislations on engine noise, emissions and braking regulations due to be introduced in April 1983 spelled the end for the Leopard, and the last chassis for the UK market were constructed in 1982 with a deadline for the vehicles to be completed by the end of March 1983.

Meeting the timeframe of this book by a mere three months is 6174 WJ, a Leopard L1/Weymann Fanfare. New to Sheffield JOC in March 1960, it subsequently passed to Midland Red but is seen here in the ownership of Hulley's of Baslow, who acquired it in 1971. Looking at the driver's mirror, you have to wonder how we coped when compared to today's 'rabbit eared' monstrosities. (RS)

Arlington Motors, the well-known bus and coach dealers, shared London Transport's Potters Bar garage, where 1960 Leopard L2 OCS 741 is seen. Fitted with a thirty-eight-seat Alexander body and new to Western SMT for the overnight Glasgow–London service, its last operator before coming south of the border was Wilson of Airdrie. (AS)

Another 1960 Leopard L2, this time fitted with Harrington's elegant Cavalier, is WWV 564. Now number 999 in the Wilts & Dorset fleet, the distinctive raised front dome is an indication that it was new to Silver Star of Porton Down. Originally fitted with forty-one coach seats, by the time this photograph was taken in Salisbury, in 1972, it had been downgraded, its bus seating visible through the windscreen. (AS)

Salisbury again, and another Harrington Cavalier/Leopard L2. New to Southdown, by 1973 8739 CD had become Western National's 2204. Seen with Royal Blue fleet names, it is surrounded by ECW-bodied Bristol REs operating a National Travel service in the days before the M4 and M5 motorways opened up the West Country. (CE)

The Duple Continental, designed by H. V. Burlingham prior to that company's takeover by Duple, was built at the former Burlingham factory in Blackpool. It only achieved modest success, but two are seen here in the yard of Walker of Hexthorpe: ex-Ribble Leopard SCK 866, fitted from new with a toilet compartment for use on London express services, and 280 HLC, an ex-Global of London AEC Reliance. (RS)

Having duplicated Sheffield United Tours' express service from Great Yarmouth, 113 EUA, a Leopard PSU3/Plaxton Embassy owned by Rosemary Coaches of Terrington St Clement in Norfolk, unloads in Sheffield bus station. Rosemary was the trading name of George Dack, who formed the company in 1957 and named it after his newborn daughter. 113 EUA was new in 1963 to Wallace Arnold and was one of several similar vehicles acquired by Dack in 1974. (RS)

Over 1,800 of Alexander's Y-type were built on Leopard chassis, of which 1,550 were delivered to Scottish operators. An early example delivered south of the border was dual-purpose 267 PRR of East Midland Motor Services, new in 1963 and seen at Doncaster Racecourse. (RS)

Along with Royal Blue, Black & White Motorways of Cheltenham was one of the six original members of Associated Motorways, formed as a result of the Road Traffic Act of 1930 which encouraged competing coach operators to co-ordinate their services. DDG 254C, a 1965 Leopard PSU3/Harrington Grenadier, is seen in Oxford's Gloucester Green bus station on an Associated Motorways working to its home town. (CE)

Following the creation of the National Bus Company, Black & White became part of National Travel (South West) along with Greenslades of Exeter, Shamrock & Rambler and Wessex of Bristol. While each fleet had its own allocation of vehicles, movements within the group were not unknown, and Leopard PSU3/Plaxton Panorama 141 (4881 DF) is seen parked in Wessex's Kingswood depot, with an original Wessex-liveried vehicle in the background. (RS)

Grey Green's CLK 472B, a 1964 Leopard PSU3/Harrington Grenadier, is seen parked at Sissinghurst Castle, Kent, in 1972. Grey Green's Grenadiers were fitted with Cavalier-style windscreens in order to accommodate the company's unusual three-track destination boxes. (CE)

In 1927, Orange Luxury Coaches built London's first dedicated coach station. It remained in use until the 1970s and was finally demolished in the 1990s. In 1953, Orange became part of the Ewer Group, owner of Grey Green, but maintained a separate identity due to holding the Royal Warrant, as seen on the side of AYL 458B, a 1964 Harrington Cavalier-bodied Leopard PSU3. Part of the 'Orange Luxury Coaches' archway can be seen to the right of the coach. (AS)

Seen unloading in its hometown bus station is Law Brothers of Sheffield's AWJ 933B, a Leopard PSU3/Plaxton Panorama delivered new in 1964. The coach met an undignified end when it ran into the back of the coach in front while returning from Skegness. Badly damaged, it was driven back to Laws' yard, where it was stripped for spares before being set on fire at the back of the depot. (RS)

Built in 1932, Black & White's St Margaret's coach station in Cheltenham was the hub of the Associated Motorways network and until closure in 1984 was famous for its 2 p.m. mass departure, initiated by the sounding of the '2 o'clock bell'. Having a rest between duties is Black & White's DDG 259C, which, despite its lower front panels, having been rebuilt at some stage, is a Leopard PSU3/Duple Commander. (RS)

DYM 453C was one of four Leopard L2/Harrington Grenadiers bought by Samuelson's New Transport in 1965. With their garage being across the road from London Victoria, they were handily placed to assist on express services calling there. However, when seen here in 1972, it was preparing to set off on one of Samuelson's own tours. (TW)

Blackpool horse carriage operator Walter Clinton Standerwick purchased his first motor bus in 1911. Following his death, his family sold the operation to Ribble Motor Services in 1932, who amalgamated all their coaching operations under the Standerwick name, this continuing until the formation of the NBC. Seen turning into London Victoria in 1973, still wearing its Standerwick livery despite now being part of the NBC, is 83 (CRN 847D), a 1966 Leopard PSU3/Plaxton Panorama. (AS)

Same location, same day, and the same sort of coach but in NBC local coach livery is Midland Red's 5832 (GHA 332D). Local coach (or dual-purpose) livery was applied to vehicles capable of fulfilling both coach and local bus work, identified by the bottom half of the vehicle being painted in the operating company's livery while the top half was painted white. (AS)

This reminds me of that joke about what's black, white and red all over. This wonderfully nostalgic shot of Trafalgar Square in 1968 shows Black & White's 283 (KDD 283E), a Leopard PSU3/Plaxton Panorama, which is closely followed by an unidentified Routemaster. (CE)

United Automobile's olive green and cream livery was used on coaches utilised on the 'Tyne–Tees–Thames' express services between the North East and London, as seen on NHN 415E, a Leopard PSU3/Plaxton Panorama. Ordered by Wilkinson of Sedgfield, it was delivered to United in 1967 after it acquired the Wilkinson business, and it is seen in Blackpool in 1972. (TW)

Neighbours Mexborough & Swinton Traction Company and Yorkshire Traction were both controlled by the BET (British Electric Traction Co.), and when the NBC was formed, Mexborough & Swinton was absorbed into Yorkshire Traction. Leopard PSU3/Duple Commander EWW 108C was one of the last coaches delivered to Mexborough & Swinton before the merger and became number 19 in the Yorkshire Traction fleet. (RS)

The cascading of ex-Southdown touring coaches to other operators within the NBC wasn't confined to the Harringtons, as this photo of Southdown's former 1201, now Bristol Omnibus 2171, shows. New in 1966, EUF 201D was photographed in the old Bath depot, where the Leopard PSU3/Plaxton Panorama was undergoing an engine change, hence the seats piled high and the side panels unlocked. (RS)

With the double N logo being the only nod towards its NBC corporate ownership, Western Welsh 169 (LUH 169F), a beautifully presented 1968 Leyland PSU3/Plaxton Panorama, arrives at London Victoria in 1973. (AS)

Dearneways of Goldthorpe's Leopard PSU3/Plaxton Panorama 70 (ULK 202F) awaits departure from Sheffield Castlegate to Thurnscoe. New to City Coach Lines of London in 1968, it passed to Dearneways in 1971. Dearneways sold it ten years later, just prior to its takeover by South Yorkshire PTE. (RS)

Seen in Douglas bus station while working the shuttle to Ronaldsway Airport are two Leopard PSU4/Duple Commander IIIs from the fleet of Corkill's Tours (Isle of Man). New to Isle of Man Road Services in 1967, they passed to Tours in 1972 as part of a restructuring which saw the bulk of IoMRS's coach operation pass to Tours. Had it not been for operational changes in 1982, which resulted in a substantial fleet reduction, it is likely that despite their age they would have survived for some time longer as they were highly regarded. (MH)

Bristol coach operator Len Munden was a fighter in more ways than one. Following a successful boxing career, cut short when he lost an arm in the RAF, he went on to successfully fight in court to be granted his PSV licence, becoming the country's first one-armed coach driver. His Crown Coaches operation took over many other Bristol operators, including Empress Coaches, whose name is carried by former Roman City of Bath Leopard PSU3/Duple Commander III FGL 393F, seen on Soundwell Road, Staple Hill. (RS)

Photographed at Edwards of Lydbrook's Gloucester depot is SRM 400G, a Leopard PSU4/Duple Commander III. It travelled well, being new to Titterington of Blencowe in 1969, and heading further north when sold by Edward's to join the fleet of Newton of Dingwall. To the right is 348 BUP, an ex-Gardiner of Spennymoor AEC Reliance, while just visible inside the garage is a Roe Dalesman. (RS)

Another short Leopard PSU4, but this time with Plaxton Panorama Elite coachwork, is TVO 981G, fleet number L05 with Gash of Newark-on-Trent. New in 1969, by the time of this photograph in Newark bus station, the body had been updated with a Plaxton Supreme IV lower front panel. (RS)

Were there an award for the most scenic bus garage, South Wales operator Creamline of Tonmawr's would have been a strong contender. Five Leopards are lined up, all but one carrying differing variants of Plaxton Panorama Elite coachwork – the odd man out on the left being a Duple Continental. (MH)

Back in the days when the UK still had a sizeable coal industry, the largest pit in north Staffordshire was Hem Heath near Trentham. Numerous operators brought in miners from the surrounding areas, including Crystal Coaches of Newcastle-under-Lyme, whose freshly re-painted Leopard PSU3/Plaxton Panorama Elite HNK 145G stands outside the canteen. (MH)

Loyal AEC operator Marchant's of Cheltenham only ran one Leyland while AECs were still available: DGC 113H, a 1970 Leopard PSU3/Plaxton Panorama Elite. The amber warning beacon just visible on the roof is a hint that its previous operator was Hall (Silverline) of Hounslow, whose operations required them to go 'airside' at Heathrow Airport. It served Marchant's for a little over two years before passing to Edmunds, Rassau, and is seen picking up in Cheltenham's Royal Well bus station. (RS)

Despite being under NBC control for over three years, Southdown's 1818 (RUF 818H) retains its operator's traditional green livery. It is one of the superb 1970 Leopard PSU3A/Duple Commander IVs fitted with just thirty-two seats for extended tours and is seen in 1973 turning into London Victoria after returning from a North Wales tour. (AS)

Córas Iompair Éireann, better known as CIÉ, is Ireland's national transport provider, and for over eighty years has operated an extensive tour programme. During the 1970s, mainland operators were contracted to supply coaches for certain tours, including World Wide Coaches, whose Leopard PSU3/Plaxton Panorama Elite ONK 649H was photographed when brand new in August 1971. Shortly afterwards it was found to be carrying the incorrect registration number and so was changed to ONK 649J. (CE)

The picturesque Derbyshire town of Bakewell is the location of Midland Red Leopard PSU3 MRF 417L, although it is not the standard NBC offering seen previously. New to Harper Bros of Heath Hayes in Staffordshire, which was acquired by Midland Red in 1974, it carries a Duple Viceroy body instead of the Commander normally found on heavyweight chassis. Added to this, at 'L' reg, Duple's Dominant range was already available, so while MRF 417L was not unique, it certainly wasn't a common combination. (MH)

Introduced in 1925, Greyhound Motors' Bristol to London service was claimed to be the first long-distance scheduled coach service. After takeover by Bristol Tramways in 1936, the Greyhound name was retained for long-distance coach services until 1972, when the NBC required Bristol to adopt the National Travel brand. Shortly before Greyhound's demise, a new service commenced between Bristol and London using the new M4 motorway, and 2157 (YHU 521J), a Leopard PSU3/Plaxton Panorama Elite, is seen in 1971 when brand new at London Victoria. (AS)

Badger racing in Bristol. Seen entering the city centre are two vehicles from the Badgerline fleet. On the left is 2106, a Plaxton Panorama Elite Express-bodied Leopard PSU3 new in 1972 to East Yorkshire, registered BKH 921K. It passed to Badgerline in 1984 and was initially re-registered VCL 461 before becoming XEU 44K. On the right is 6000 (DAE 510W), one of five Rolls-Royce-engined MCW Metrobuses delivered to Bristol Omnibus Co. in 1980. When new, all five had different all-over advertising liveries promoting discount travel cards. (RS)

SELNEC (South East Lancashire, North East Cheshire) PTE was formed in 1970 and absorbed the majority of north-west England's municipal and corporation bus fleets. Seen in Manchester Victoria bus station is Plaxton Panorama Elite Express-bodied Leopard 74 (XNE 885L), one of a batch of six delivered new to SELNEC in 1973. (RS)

Numerous operators across the country were absorbed into the Wallace Arnold empire, and a small number of vehicles carried the acquired operator's name incorporated into the standard Wallace Arnold livery. Seen at Doncaster Racecourse displaying the Gillard's of Normanton name is Leopard PSU3/Plaxton Panorama Elite KUM 539L from 1973. (RS)

One of the first continental bodybuilders to make inroads into the UK market was Belgian company Van Hool. In 1972, Essex operator Harris of Grays took delivery of SVX 799K, a Leopard PSU3 with Van Hool's Vistadome coachwork, and entered it into that year's Brighton Coach Rally. (AS)

Quite a head-turner when it was new in 1974 to Turner's of Bristol was SHY 707M, a 12-metre Leopard PSU5/Van Hool Vistadome. It is parked in Sussex Street, St Phillips, in what was once the view from my traffic office window in the area known as Bristol's coaching triangle, as Wessex of Bristol, Turner's and Munden's Crown Coaches were all based within half a mile of each other. (RS)

While Van Hool went from strength to strength, other continentals were not so successful. Before attempting to crack the UK market in the early 1980s with the spectacularly unsuccessful Magirus Deutz-based Apollo and Diana bodies, Spain's Ayats bodied a 12-metre Leopard PSU5 for London-based David Corbel. Marketed through Northern Ireland-based Asco, JJD 802N was to remain unique, and is seen here when brand new taking part in the 1975 Brighton Coach rally. (AS)

CIÉ's 'M' class PSU5 Leopards were all fitted with the operator's own bodywork, with a mix of dual-purpose and coach interiors across the 200-strong class. Many were re-engined in the late 1970s, some receiving DAF units, and others (including Expressway-liveried M118) General Motors two-stroke engines. M118 is seen outside Dublin's central bus station on the dock shuttle service in 1978 and, despite looking rather down at heel, lasted a further twenty years before being scrapped in 1998 – a career of nearly twenty-eight years. (MH)

Alexander's M-type was a luxurious body built almost exclusively for the Scottish Bus Group's Anglo-Scottish services. Fitted with oil-fired heating, a toilet and in most cases seating for only forty-two passengers, their trapezoid windows were an attempt to emulate the American Greyhound coaches. The only M-type not to go to the SBG was RTF 561L, a Leopard PSU5 delivered to Ribble in 1973. By the time this picture was taken in London Victoria in 1982 it had passed to National Travel West. (AS)

In the days when coach stations seemed to be full of nothing but National Travel's white coaches, the SBG fleets, each with their individual colour schemes, were a breath of fresh air. Northern Scottish, with its attractive yellow and cream livery, was formed in 1985 from Walter Alexander & Sons (Northern) Ltd. Two of its Alexander M-type PSU5 Leopards, with NPE32 (GSO 532N) closest to the camera, are about to depart London Victoria for Aberdeen in 1975. (AS)

As with NBC, the SBG subsidiaries succumbed to a corporate livery, with coaches painted blue and white complete with a large saltire. New to Fife in 1975, by 1982, when it was photographed pulling into London Victoria, Leopard PSU5/Alexander M-type HSG 565N had become NPE37 in the Northern Scottish fleet. (AS)

New to Teesside Municipal Transport along with a Duple Dominant and a Plaxton Panorama Elite as part of an evaluation programme for its private hire fleet, KXG 372L was a Leopard PSU3 fitted with a Willowbrook Expressway body. Later in life it was downgraded and fitted with bus seats, and in 1986 it was rebodied. By the time this photo was taken, Teesside had become Cleveland Transit. (RS)

Issues with build quality, not improved by the huge side windows and narrow frames, didn't help the Willowbrook Expressway, and only about 150 were built. Tyne & Wear PTE took a batch in 1973, including Leopard PSU3 1807 (LVK 407L), seen at Doncaster Racecourse on hire to Armstrong's, which had recently been acquired by the PTE. (RS)

Leopards were very much a minority in the Great Yarmouth-based Caroline Seagull fleet, but two prepare to set out with a tour from the seafront. PSU3/Plaxton Panorama Elites BPT 670L and RUP 386M were both new to County Durham independent Trimdon Motor Services. They were almost a matching pair apart from trim differences and repositioned emergency exits differentiating between the Elite II and Elite III. (MH)

Good job there's a badge or two to tell you what this is! Back in the 1980s many operators added new Supreme IV front ends onto ageing Plaxton Panorama Elites to make them look more modern. With the addition of a dateless registration, they appeared to the public (outwardly at least) to be a modern coach. Seen at Chester Zoo during 1989, 7222 EL (formerly HWU 66N and new to Wallace Arnold) and the Leopard/Plaxton Viewmaster to its left belonged to Ron Lyles & Son of Batley, West Yorkshire. (MH)

The picturesque Oxfordshire village of Charlton-on-Otmoor is the home to Holder's Charlton Services, which operates a network of rural services in the Oxford and Banbury areas. Seen in Charlton High Street just down from the depot is Leopard PSU3/ Plaxton Panorama Elite Express GUD 708L, new to the company in 1972, where it remained for a commendable twenty-four years until sold in 1996. (RJ)

Barton of Chilwell took nearly 200 Leopards, all bodied by Plaxton. From the early 1970s, Barton standardised on new coaches for all its purchases, all built to Express specification. By this time, Barton was Britain's largest independent bus and coach operator, and used coaches on all of its local services, as well as on tours and express work. 1420 (PNN 774M) is about to call at Doncaster South bus station on its marathon journey to Glasgow. If the sight of a Mk 4 Cortina estate doesn't make you feel nostalgic then don't look at the price of fuel! (RS)

Greater Manchester PTE's private hire division operated under the Charterplan, Godfrey Abbot, Lancashire United Coaches and Warburton's banners. While a common livery style and fleet name font were used, each company had their individual colours on the side stripes. Showing the two-tone blue used for the Warburton's fleet is 95 (JND 995N), a 1975 Leopard PSU3/Duple Dominant seen at Windsor coach park in 1978. (AS)

Looking more a combination of parts than a designed body, the East Lancs Lancastrian had a production run of three. One was built on a Seddon chassis for Hyndburn, while the other two were on Leopard PSU3 chassis for Halton. The second of the Halton pair was 9 (JFV 295N), a 1975 Leopard PSU3B seen approaching Wembley Stadium in 1981. In 1983, both were rebodied with East Lancs bus bodies. (AS)

A coach I did a fair few miles in when it transferred to Western National from Midland Red was Leopard PSU3/Duple Dominant 2431 (PCW 675P), new to Ribble in 1976. Its usual haunt was the one-vehicle Canworthy Water outstation, but during the summer it would be used on National Express duplicates, usually to Plymouth but sometimes getting as far as the heady heights of Bristol – not bad for a thirteen-year-old Leopard! Withdrawn in 1991, it is seen at the depot of much-missed Cornish independent Willis of Bodmin, who kept withdrawn vehicles around the depot perimeter. (MH)

Gloucestershire-based Castleway's of Winchcombe was renowned for the presentation of its vehicles, immaculately turned out in a discreet dark blue and grey livery. It was quick to order one of the new Plaxton Supreme bodies when Leopard PSU3 MDF 112P arrived in 1976. Fitted with the Express variant of the Supreme, complete with split-leaf entrance doors, it remained with Castleway's for fourteen years before passing to Paul S. Winson of Loughborough. (RS)

Love it or hate it, Plaxton's Viewmaster was a striking looking body, and was essentially a standard Supreme raised by approximately 10 inches. It was created following discussions at the 1975 Nice Coach Rally between Manchester operator Tatlock's of Radcliffe and Plaxton's about producing a high-floor luxury coach. The first one was fitted to a Leopard PSU5 chassis and delivered to Tatlock's a year later. Tatlock's also received OBN 533R, the second Viewmaster built, and it is seen here taking part in the Brighton Coach Rally in 1977. (AS)

As well as the luxurious M-Type, Alexander's also built more utilitarian bodies, including the T-type, intended more as a dual-purpose vehicle than a full coach. New in 1976, PWW 708R of West Riding is seen in Wakefield. (RS)

The National Express 'venetian blind' livery of alternating blue and red stripes was adapted by NBC operating companies for coaches not used on National Express work. Western National chose the Cornish colours of black and gold for their Cornwall Coachways unit, as seen on another of my old drives, 3508 (SFJ 158R), a 1977 Leopard PSU3 Plaxton Supreme Express seen in Parliament Square, Westminster, on a private hire in 1984. (AS)

For the UK market, the next model to come out of Van Hool's Belgian factory after the Vistadome was the Aragon. Only seven were put onto Leopards, and Horlock's Coaches of Northfleet, Kent, operated two of them, one being acquired second-hand from Travellers of Hounslow, and CTM 417T, which was delivered new. It is seen when brand new in 1979 on Hampton Court station forecourt carrying Granby Travel Services livery. (RC)

Willowbrook's next offering after the Expressway was the 008 Spacecar, or 'plastic pig' as they were affectionately known. Unlike anything that had been seen before (or probably since for that matter ...), their futuristic looks saw them allocated to prestigious work where looks were more of a requirement than substance. VDH 243S was delivered in 1977 to National Travel West for use as the team coach for West Bromwich Albion, and was fitted with just twenty-eight seats, tables, full catering facilities and a television. (AS)

Sister coach VDH 244S was similarly equipped but employed as the team coach for neighbouring Wolverhampton Wanderers FC and is seen bringing the team into Wembley Stadium for their League Cup final fixture against Nottingham Forest in 1980. The Wolves players obviously appreciated the niceties of 1970s plastic and soft trim as they won the match 1-0. (AS)

Included to show how quickly the Spacecar became battle-scarred is REL 400R, seen departing Bristol Marlborough Street bus station in 1983 when only six years old. New to Shamrock & Rambler in 1977, the Willowbrook body lasted less than ten years before it was replaced by a Plaxton Derwent bus body and passed to Graham's of Paisley. (RS)

Privatisation of the NBC saw the previously plain white coaches outshopped in a myriad of new colourful liveries. Leopard PSU3/Plaxton Supreme 3516 (VOD 616S) was one of a small fleet of coaches kept at Newquay by the newly privatised Western National to operate day tours and National Express duplicates and is seen travelling down Narrowcliffe in its home town. (MH)

During busy periods, coaches more suitable to local work would be pressed into use on longer distance express services. Fife Scottish FPE133 (GSG 133T), a 1978 Leopard PSU3 with very late Duple Dominant I Express body, makes an unusual sight at London Victoria in 1981 after having duplicated an Anglo-Scottish service. Immaculately presented, with wheel trims front and rear, it would usually be used on tours and inter-urban work out of St Andrew's depot. (AS)

When Britain's coach services were deregulated in October 1980, a consortium of independent coach operators formed British Coachways to compete with National Express and the SBG. Most vehicles remained in their owners' livery, but a small number received British Coachways colours, as shown on Wallace Arnold's CED 203T, a 1978 Leopard PSU3/Duple Dominant II parked in Kings Cross coach station, London, in 1981. (AS)

Wallace Arnold was one of the driving forces in British Coachways; however, falling passenger numbers caused in no small part by the inability to use recognised departure points in major cities saw it leave the consortium in the summer of 1981. A month prior to this, a pair of PSU5 Leopard/Plaxton Supreme IVs, LUA 285V and PNW 296W, are seen on what is now the site of the British Library, about to set off to opposite ends of the country from Kings Cross. (AS)

Mountain Goat achieved a degree of fame by operating a Bedford OB on heritage sightseeing tours of the English Lake District, but more relevant to this publication is enthusiastically driven UCS 858S, a Leopard PSU3/Plaxton Supreme new to Clyde Coast. Seen swinging out of The Crescent into English Street in Carlisle, I'd love to know what the sign in the foreground was prohibiting. (MH)

Tatlock's continued to show its commitment to the Viewmaster project, taking a further Leopard PSU5, this time with the newer Viewmaster IV body but without the driver's bunks specified on the previous examples. WBN 10T was delivered in 1979 and is being put thought its paces at that year's Brighton Coach Rally. (AS)

Delivered new to Bedminster Coaches of Bristol, WHW 465T was a 12-metre PSU5 with one of the last of the original Plaxton Supreme bodies. Seen in Blackpool, it subsequently passed to Julian Blundell's Duchy Tours of Camborne, Cornwall. It was well liked by its drivers due to being fitted with a Webasto heater and two-speed axle. (RS)

When is a tiger not a tiger? When it's a Leopard! One of the more entertaining liveries applied to NBC coaching units was that used by Trent for its Trent Tigers coaching unit (they even took a batch of Leyland Tigers with GRR registrations). YRC 182 (originally CVO 3T) was a 1979 Leopard PSU3/Plaxton Supreme IV and is seen arriving at Wembley Stadium in 1989. (AS)

Its network of express services radiating from East Anglia made Premier Travel of Cambridge a familiar sight on the roads of Britain. Premier standardised on the AEC Reliance but switched to the Leopard when Reliance production ended. Together with Yelloway of Rochdale, another diehard Reliance operator, it persuaded Leyland to make the Leopard available with a ZF manual gearbox rather than the usual semi-automatic offering. BVA 789V was the last of the first batch of Leopards, and the last Premier vehicle, to be painted in the blue livery. (CE)

From the next batch of Leopards onwards, all Premier coaches were painted in a silver and blue livery, complete with large logo reflecting Premier's status as a travel group rather than just a coach company, its portfolio including a travel agency and travel shops. Seen departing Heathrow Central bus station en route to its home city is CJE 453V. All of Premier's Leopards were 11-metre PSU3s. (RC)

Nearly half way through before I've managed to get a Yelloway photo in, but that's because it didn't take its first Leopards until 1980, the company policy of always buying British leaving it no alternative once production of its beloved AEC Reliance had ceased. CTD 134V, a PSU5/Plaxton Supreme, was one of the first, and as with the Premier examples was fitted with a ZF six-speed manual gearbox. It is seen in Plymouth Bretonside bus station, ready to depart for home. (JL)

As well as providing coaches for National Express services, NBC subsidiaries were expected to provide them for National Holidays work, whether it be day trips or extended tours. PSU5/ Duple Dominant II JDG 283V was a member of the Devon-based Greenslades division of National Travel (South West), and it is seen in its home city of Exeter while operating an All British Tour. Good to see that care and attention had been paid when the no smoking stickers were applied. (RJ)

Being based in East Ham, Lacey's was the natural choice to supply the team coach to West Ham United. Although not the actual team coach, Leopard PSU5/Plaxton Supreme IV MNM 39V was used regularly enough as a supporters' coach to have the club name on its destination blind. It is seen when brand new at Pyecombe on the old A23. (AS)

In 1980, to find a suitable replacement chassis for its fleet of leased AEC Reliances, London Country took a pair of Leopard PSU3/Duple Dominants to be evaluated against a pair of Volvo B58s. All were put to work on the northern orbital Green Line route 734. The Leopards won the day and a further thirty were ordered, again on a five-year lease with the bodies split equally between Duple and Plaxton. (DJ)

The least successful of Duple's Dominant range was the Dominant III, the pillars between the trapezoid windows being so thick that some passengers had no view out of the coach at all. An unusual vehicle in the Potteries fleet was Leopard PSU3 KWG 131W, which arrived from Excelsior of Dinnington via Turner of Brown Edge when that business was acquired by Potteries. Carrying rather rudimentary branding for service 23 to Sheffield, it was withdrawn in 2000 but is now preserved. (RS)

To me, some of the finest Leopards to grace the roads were the thirteen Plaxton Supreme V-bodied PSU5s delivered to National Travel (South West) in 1981. SND 293X was allocated to the Wessex of Bristol fleet and, unusually for a coach, received all-over advertising. Useless trivia time – Radio West was Bristol's first independent radio station, formed in 1981, a year after the BBC drama series *Shoestring* ended. The central character in *Shoestring* was a Bristol-based private eye who worked at a radio station called … Radio West. (RS)

Another Dominant III, but this time a PSU5 complete with the shallower windscreen required due to the fitting of a headboard box. Beeston's of Hadleigh had a batch of eight, all lettered for different companies within the Beeston group, and having a slight identity crisis between Mulley's and Comb's is WGV 895X, seen about to depart Angel Hill, Bury St Edmunds, on a local bus service. (RS)

The B51 body was developed by ECW at the request of the NBC, which wanted to rebody older ECW-bodied Bristol REs to make a cheap dual-purpose coach. After the prototype was built, the plan was changed and the B51 body was only fitted to brand-new Leopard and Tiger chassis. VUD 33X of City of Oxford was a 1982 Leopard PSU3 and is seen at High Wycombe bus station in 1988. (AS)

Soon after its introduction, structural problems were discovered with the rear ends of the B51 body, which caused them to sag and crack. They were either returned to ECW for repair or had strengthening work carried out in-house. OWJ 166X of Yorkshire Traction was caught leaving Barnsley on Service X34 to Sheffield. (RS)

Willowbrook's last real foray into mainstream coachbuilding was with the 003, another no-frills body designed primarily as a cheap coach for the NBC, which took 227 out of the 231 built. All but a handful were built on the Leopard PSU3 chassis. DDM 22X was new in 2981 to Crosville as its ELL22 but is seen here in Louth bus station in the ownership of Grimsby-Cleethorpes Transport. (RS)

KET 161W was one of a pair of Willowbrook 003s new in 1981 to Yorkshire Traction, which was so unimpressed with the build quality that both were transferred to fellow NBC subsidiary South Midland at the first opportunity. (RS)

Three Leopards from the South Yorkshire PTE coaching unit are lined up in age order while on a private hire: Duple Dominant 1069 (MWJ 469P), which, already third hand, was new to National Travel (East) and passed to SYPTE from Dearneways; Plaxton Supreme IV Express 1093 (AWJ 293T), which was new to Dearneways; and the very late Duple Dominant 1 Express 17 (JKW 217W), which was new to the PTE. (RS)

NBC subsidiaries rarely acquired second-hand vehicles unless through company takeovers, but Midland Red (East) 71 was one such purchase. Midland Red had ordered three Plaxton Paramount 3200-bodied Tigers in 1983, but they were diverted to Western National and Devon General. In exchange, Western National transferred a Leopard, but Devon General had nothing suitable so, by some convoluted process, this PSU5 Leopard was supplied. HHW 471X, with a late Supreme IV body complete with stainless steel lower mouldings, was new to Bedminster Coaches of Bristol in 1981. (RS)

A lovely example of the Duple Dominant IV, the last incarnation of the Dominant range is SHD 330X. Fitted with fifty reclining seats and double glazing throughout, it was new to Hodder of Clitheroe, but soon passed to Essex-based Boon's of Boreham. Somehow, the minimalist side and front mouldings and flat rather than curved side windows made the Dominant IV appear more elegant than the earlier models in the range. (RJ)

The Supreme VI with its shallow side windows was the least successful model in the Plaxton Supreme range, only being produced between 1981 and 1982, with less than a handful fitted onto Leopard chassis. DFE 361X was delivered new in 1982 to Eagre of Gainsborough and is seen in Gainsborough bus station operating the cross-town service between Lea and Morton. (RS)

Even fewer Leopards were bodied from new with Plaxton Paramount bodies. The chassis of 9962R (originally LVL 727Y) was built in 1979 but it was not bodied until 1983, and it is unusual in being a low-height Paramount 3200 fitted with the full-height rear continental door more usually fitted to the higher Paramount 3500. It was delivered new to Eagre in 1983 and when photographed in Gainsborough bus station had received an updated front end. (RS)

The Panther

By the early part of the 1960s, manufacturers were designing rear-engined single-deck chassis suitable for both bus and coach work, and at the 1964 Earls Court Motor Show, Leyland launched the Panther. While only offered with an 18-foot 6-inch wheelbase, two separate versions were available: the PSUR1.1 for bus work and the PSUR1.2, which was intended mainly for coaching activities. In order to obtain a degree of commonality, it was decided to use the same chassis frames for both the Panther and for AEC's new rear-engined bus, the Swift, but unlike the Swift, the Panther had a front-mounted radiator, helping to alleviate the overheating issues that dogged the Southall product. However, it was with the Leopard that the Panther shared a closer relationship as both shared the same pneumocyclic gearbox and 0.600 engine, both mounted behind the rear axle. The Panther bus had a low chassis from the front of the vehicle which then stepped up over the engine and gearbox at a point just ahead of the rear axle. This allowed bodybuilders to create a body offering wide one-step entry and exit doors with a flat floor for most of the vehicle. The coach version had a straight chassis frame which rose gradually from front to rear, and as the traditional luggage area at the rear of the coach was now occupied by the engine, most of the area between the axles was available for luggage storage, which was accessible from both sides of the vehicle. Shortly after the Panther was announced, Leyland offered a full air suspension system as an option, along with dual line air brakes, a two-speed rear axle and the 0.680 engine for the coach version.

While the PSUR1.2 as a coach sold moderately well overseas, only twenty-four PSUR1.2 chassis were bodied as coaches for the UK market. It was unfortunate for the Panther, with its advanced technical specification, that it had the Leopard as its 'zoo-mate'. As operators were still getting used to the myriad of new legislation that had been introduced in the last decade, they appeared to be rather conservative when it came to vehicle buying, preferring to stick to the tried and tested. Only four operators purchased Panther coaches in the UK, the first being delivered to Gloucestershire independent Soudley Valley Coaches in 1966 while the last two were delivered to Skill's of Nottingham in 1971. The largest batch of Panther coaches was ordered by Luton-based Seamark's Coaches, which took sixteen complete with 0.680 engines, full air suspension and fitted with televisions, and East Yorkshire Motor Services took five, including two with unusual MCW Topaz bodywork.

The final Panthers were built in 1972, and while its production run was probably one of the shortest of the post-war Leyland models, the practical experience it gave Leyland was to prove invaluable when the next generation of rear-engined single-deck vehicles was introduced later that same year.

Only twenty-four Panther coaches were built for the UK market, with the first delivered to Soudley Valley Coaches of Cinderford in 1967. Plaxton Panorama-bodied KDF 743E is seen in 1976 on King Edward's Parade, Eastbourne. (AS)

East Yorkshire Motor Services operated five Panther coaches as well as nineteen Panther buses. The first two coaches were fitted with unusual MCW Topaz II bodies and were delivered in 1967. 823 (JRH 323E) is seen in full NBC corporate livery at Wembley Stadium. (AS)

East Yorkshire's remaining three coaches were fitted with more conventional forty-seven-seat Plaxton Panorama bodies, as seen on 849 (MRH 849F). Delivered in 1968, it is seen arriving at London Victoria in 1973. The Panthers were not the most successful coaches EYMS operated, and most were withdrawn after nine years' service. (AS)

Eastbourne seems to have been a popular place to send Panthers, as Seamark's Plaxton Panorama-bodied SXD 471F is seen when brand new in Susan's Road, passing the town's railway station. With a total of sixteen vehicles delivered between 1968 and 1969, Seamark's operated the largest fleet of Panther coaches in the UK. (AS)

Being Luton-based, Seamark's was ideally located for undertaking airport transfers, and the Panthers with their rapid turn of speed combined with excellent fuel economy made them ideal for the job. Reliability, however, was another matter and led to their premature withdrawal, with operators such as Bicester-based Grayline snapping them up. Seen in 1980 sandwiched between two Plaxton-bodied brethren – an unidentified Bedford VAL and Leopard RTU 556L – is SXD 467F, which arrived in 1972, with SXD 474/6F coming a year later. (MH)

The ex-Seamark's Panthers seemed to have had a knack of sticking together, as SXD 474/6F were sold by Grayline to Bere Regis, where they joined SXD 473F, seen here in 1979 parked at Bristol Docks. They had relatively long lives in Dorset, SXD 474F remaining on site as a store shed until broken for scrap in 1990. (AS)

Seamark's drivers remember the Panthers as being fantastic motors, and with their semi-automatic gearboxes, rear engines and air suspension, they were felt to be ahead of their time. The 'F' registered vehicles were retro-fitted with two-speed rear axles, while the 'G' registered vehicles were factory fitted and were reputed to be good for over 90 mph. SXD 475F, now with Simmond's of Hillingdon, looks a little bit past the days of achieving such feats. (RJ)

The list of interesting vehicles operated by Cornish independent Trelawney Tours of Hayle would make mildly interesting reading (the idea for another book springs to mind ...), and when SXD 468F was pride of the fleet, its stablemates included an ex-Provincial Seddon Pennine IV, an ex-Cardiff Alexander-bodied AEC Swift and an ex-Black & White Daimler Roadliner. (MH)

I know what you're thinking, but it's not what it looks like. Marazion, on the outskirts of Penzance, is home to Mount's Bay Coaches and St Michael's Mount. VXE 278G, from Seamark's second batch of Panthers, has acquired the front panel from an AEC Reliance; the question is, had the badge been welded onto the grille, or had Mount's Bay's owner Mr Oxenham regretted buying the Panther? Another poser is why the depot building is lettered for a company from Birmingham. While the entrance has been widened and the road tarmacked, Mount's Bay's depot is little changed today; even the lettering on the building remains. (MH)

The only Panthers to carry Plaxton Panorama Elite bodies were the four operated by Skill's of Nottingham, and 69 (XAU 69J) was the penultimate Panther coach to enter service in the UK. With Doncaster Racecourse as the location, AW 3321 – the Super Sentinel steam waggon in the background – can still be seen on the steam rally scene today. (RS)

The Panthers could hold 70 mph on a motorway all day long, but stopping was another thing, drivers recalling that pressing the brake pedal was akin to standing on a brick. Another negative memory was the lack of room between seat and steering wheel, making things uncomfortable for taller drivers. With 69 by its side, 70 (XAU 70J) is seen just after delivery in 1970. (RS)

Fitting destination glasses underneath the windscreens meant the Panther badge had to be relocated; in my eyes fitting it to the lower rather than upper grille would have been more aesthetically pleasing. By 1982, RTV 668G (retaining the earlier more colourful Skill's livery albeit with rather crude fleet name removal) had passed to Border of Barnoldswick and was parked in London Victoria, preparing to undertake a National Express duplicate to Burnley. (JL)

The Tiger

Leyland needed to address the influx of high specification continental chassis entering the UK market, and with legislation putting the writing on the wall for the Leopard, a new chassis had to be built to protect Leyland's market share. In 1981 Leyland announced Project B43 and, reviving a name from its past, called it the Tiger. The Tiger was a radical change from the Leopard, having full air suspension, a turbocharged engine and a choice of manual or semi-automatic gearboxes, as well as a completely redesigned driver's area with car-like controls and that luxury of luxuries – a fuel gauge on the dashboard. The Tiger was launched in a blaze of glory at an event reputed to have cost over £1 million and held in Gibraltar and Tangier, Morocco.

The Tiger was initially only available with the newly launched turbocharged TL11 engine, a development of the 0.680. Output was 218 bhp but a 245 bhp option was made available shortly afterwards and in 1984 this was increased again to produce 260 bhp. 1984 also saw Leyland offer the Gardner 6HLXC engine, aimed primarily at the Scottish Bus Group, which had an unwillingness to use Leyland engines, much preferring the Gardner product (as seen in the large number of Seddon Pennines operated, Seddon more than happy to fit the Gardner into their vehicles). Leyland initially refused to offer the Gardner engine, but after Dennis introduced the Gardner-engined Dorchester aimed specifically at the SBG market and started to sell it in good numbers north of the border, Leyland relented and the Patricroft product was added to the Tiger options. The Tiger chassis required modifications due to the Gardner being significantly larger than the TL11, and while the Dorchester threat was successfully avoided, the market for Gardner-engined Tigers outside of the SBG was limited. A further engine option was added in 1987 when the 290 bhp Cummins L10 was made available, usually paired with a ZF gearbox. By now the Tiger was a serious competitor to Volvo's B10M, which was still outselling the home market product.

With the sale of Leyland Bus to Volvo, the UK's two best-selling coaches, the Tiger and the B10M, came under common ownership; however, Volvo had the foresight to see that the Tiger had a loyal customer base as well as a good reputation, and so the two models continued in production side by side. By 1989, the Tiger was offered with the Volvo THD100 engine as fitted to the B10M and the TL11 and Gardner options were dropped, leaving only Cummins and Volvo as engine options. Two years later, in 1991, Shearings Holidays, which was one of the major purchasers of the Tiger, switched allegiance to the Volvo B10M, and with sales of the Tiger declining, the model was dropped from the catalogue, bringing the production of Leyland coaches to an end.

New as FRN 816W, MSV 927 was the first Tiger demonstrator and took part in the model's launch event in Morocco. Originally fitted with a 218 bhp engine and pneumocyclic gearbox, it was later uprated to 245 bhp with hydracyclic gearbox. After its demonstration days were over it joined the fleet of Gash, Newark, later becoming 1417 in the Lincolnshire Road Car fleet when Gash's was taken over. It is seen here in St Mark's bus station, Lincoln. (RS)

Anticipating the competition that deregulation of express services would bring, the SBG placed a pre-production order for eight Tigers, one of which took part in the lavish Moroccan launch event. They were the first vehicles fitted with the Duple Dominant III body, which Duple designed specifically for the SBG order before making it generally available. Seen a month after delivery at London Victoria is Eastern Scottish XH549 (BSG 549W). (AS)

The next Tiger coaches bought by the SBG for Anglo-Scottish services were fitted with the new highline version of the Dominant – the Goldliner. The Goldliner was a heavy body, and with only 218 bhp on tap, these elegant-looking coaches were woefully underpowered. Eastern Scottish Goldliner IV XH554A (MSC 554X) is seen pulling into London Victoria in 1982. (AS)

As with Plaxton's Viewmaster, the Duple Goldliner was a raised version of the standard height body, in this case the Dominant. This became obvious when no destination boxes were fitted, resulting in a stepped roofline immediately behind the door. Seen on a wintry morning is BLH 717Y, a Goldliner III delivered to Hamilton of Uxbridge. (RJ)

Talking of the Viewmaster, some of the earliest Tigers were under that very body, but as it was soon to be replaced with the new Paramount range, they were relatively rare. British Airways took delivery of six 11-metre examples in 1981/2, all to Express specification for crew transfer work at Heathrow and Manchester. C313 (VOY 180X) is seen at Heathrow Central when brand new. (AS)

Italian coachbuilder Padane attempted to make inroads into the UK market with the striking ZX body. Unfortunately, it was both expensive and heavy, and only ten were imported through Grays-based dealers Ensign – two on Mercedes chassis, seven on Volvo B10Ms and one on a Tiger. XPP 289X is seen at the 1982 British Coach Rally. (SG)

The launch of the Tiger was too late in the year for many operators to place an order for delivery for the 1981 season, but for 1982 it hit the road running, so to speak. Rees & Williams, Tycroes, took two, including MCY 839X with Plaxton Supreme V Express coachwork. (RS)

London Country operated the largest fleet of Tigers in the UK, with nearly 300 fitted with a variety of bodies. One of the first to be delivered was TL4 (TPC 104X), which was fitted with an ECW B51 body and liveried for the 757 Flightline service between Luton and London. It is seen turning into Eccleston Street, Victoria, in 1982. Most of this early batch of ECW-bodied Tigers were rebodied with East Lancs bus bodies when less than ten years old. (AS)

Picking up in Wellington Street coach station, Leeds, is Duple Dominant IV-bodied Tiger NVH 961X. It was new to Stanley Gath of Dewsbury, which was one of the earliest non-NBC operators to undertake regular contracted National Express work rather than duplicate operations. (RS)

After trying the Leopard for two seasons, Premier Travel took the plunge and ordered five Plaxton Supreme V Express-bodied Tigers for delivery at the start of 1982. 294 (VAV256X) is seen at Hopton in Feb 1987 undertaking the 0630 hrs Cambridge–Lowestoft service, which returned with the 1100 hrs Lowestoft–Bristol service. By this time, Premier vehicles had started to carry National Express livery for the jointly operated group of services. (CE)

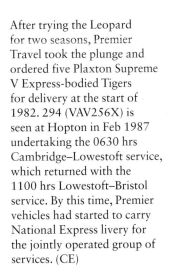

OK Motor Services was founded in Evenwood, County Durham, by Wade Emmerson in 1912.
Bishop Auckland was the main garage, with further depots at Heaton, Newcastle, St Helens
Auckland and Shotton Colliery (acquired with the business of F. Lockey & Sons). Most of OK's
services operated in south Tyne & Wear and Durham. By 1994 it had 212 vehicles with an
average age of eleven years, having bought forty-seven new vehicles the previous year. Seen in
Newcastle is LFT4X, an 11-metre Tiger/Plaxton Supreme V Express. (RC)

As with neighbouring Greater Manchester PTE, Merseyside PTE also had a coaching arm, and
took delivery of twelve Duple Dominant IV-bodied Tigers in 1982. With privatisation of the
PTEs, it was rebranded as Merseycoach and 7016 (EKA 216Y) is seen arriving at Wembley
Stadium with St Helens fans on the occasion of the 1987 Rugby League Challenge Cup. (AS)

With the Tiger being launched late in 1981 and Duple replacing the Dominant range in 1982, only a handful of NBC operators received Dominant-bodied Tiger coaches. Oxford/South Midland received a batch of ten for the busy Oxford–London motorway express service, and EBW 109Y is seen departing Gloucester Green bus station, Oxford, for the capital in 1983. (CE)

One of the many body styles carried by London Country's Tigers was the Dominant IV. With the same body as the Oxford Tiger above, moving the destination box level with the roofline rather than in a 'Bristol dome' radically alters the frontal appearance of the coach. One of ten fitted with forty-six reclining seats and originally used on the Jetlink 747 service, TD32 (YPD 132Y) was operating a National Holidays tour when caught in Plymouth Bretonside bus station in 1985. (RC)

Seen with what appears to be the world's longest Mercedes minibus in the background is Duple Dominant IV-bodied 260 ERY (originally carried by a Leicester City Transport Leyland PD2). It was another former Welsh Tiger which had stealthily crept its way up to Powell's of Hellaby, being new in 1982 as NTG 18X to Morris of Pencoed. (RS)

From humble beginnings running from a rented yard in Brentford, Armchair grew to be one of the largest privately owned bus and coach operators in London. Specialising in the incoming tourist market, all coaches were built to Armchair's specification, which included orange seats and orange destination blinds on both sides of the coach as well as the front. Armchair purchased its first five Tigers in early 1982, including XPP 294X, which carried additional badging on the sides as it was used by Leyland in a promotional advert for the Tiger. (RJ)

After coming off lease in 1988, WPH 132Y, the former London Country TL32, was one of a number of similar vehicles that passed to Chartercoach of Harwich for use on National Express contracts. It is seen turning into London Victoria in 1988, a month into its new ownership. (AS)

Eastern National Alexander TE-bodied Tiger A696 OHJ brazenly leaves Folkstone bus station in clear contravention of the sign saying East Kent vehicles only! Following the deregulation of coach services in 1980, Eastern National introduced a series of long-distance services under the Highwayman banner. The Alexander T-type came in three versions: TS (stage), TE (express) and TC (coach). During its six-year production run, 234 were built, forty of which were delivered to the NBC. (MH)

Plaxton replaced the Supreme with the Paramount in 1983, and these were initially available as the low-height 3200 and highline 3500 versions. One of the largest coach operators in South Wales was Hill's of Tredegar, which took a batch of Paramount 3200 Express-bodied Tigers very early in the production run, RNY 305Y being the seventh Express body built. (AS)

London-based Frames-Rickards was formed in 1967 when Charles Rickards (Tours) Ltd became a subsidiary of Frames Tours Ltd, both being old established coach operators. In 1894 Charles Rickards was appointed as Posting Master to Queen Victoria and in 1936 was awarded the Royal Warrant, and this was retained when the new company was formed. The Royal Crest can be seen proudly displayed on Paramount 3200 Tiger JNM 756Y and Leopard Plaxton Supreme IV KBH 847V, both seen parked at Hampton Court station in 1984. (SG)

NBC subsidiaries were early recipients of the Paramount, kitted out to standard and executive specification. The latter were for the recently introduced 'Rapide' services, which featured hostess service, at-seat catering and onboard entertainment. Black & White (now under the umbrella of National Travel West) took ten 3200 Paramounts in 1983, including Rapide spec 215 (CDG 215Y), seen waiting at the top end of London Victoria, surrounded by NBC variety in the form of a dual-purpose Leopard/Duple Dominant of Crosville and ECW B51 Tigers of Oxford. (RJ)

Seen parked outside the Union Hotel in the pretty Cotswold village of Northleach while operating the long cross-country 747 service from Bristol to Clacton is Premier Travel's Paramount 3200 297 (FAV 564Y). Premier's vehicles were fitted with an unusual three-track destination box, and as a paper label for Cambridge, Premier's home city, is attached to the front windscreen, it must be assumed that the centre blind on 297 was defective. (CE)

The service between Oxford and London is the most intensive coach service in Britain, and while nowadays it is hotly contested between Oxford Tube and the Oxford Bus Company, prior to deregulation City of Oxford was the sole operator on the route. The NBC 'venetian blind' style livery was adapted for the Oxford Citylink operation, as seen on two Plaxton Paramount-bodied Tigers waiting to depart from Oxford's Gloucester Green bus station. 3500-bodied 121 (B121 UUD) is on the X70 to Heathrow Airport while 3200-bodied 114 (A114 MUD), on the right, is on the 190 to London. Note the subtle differences to the frontal styling between the Mk 1 and 2 Paramounts. (SG)

Duple introduced its replacement range for the Dominant and Goldliner at the same time that Plaxton introduced the Paramount and this range too featured low and highline models. Unlike the Paramount, the low-height Laser and highline Caribbean bore no resemblance to each other, the Laser being aerodynamically designed, while the Caribbean was much more angular. Laser-bodied Tiger C499 FAX was new to Henley's of Abertillery in 1986 and stayed in the South Wales fleet until 2013. (MH)

Better known for its extensive tour operations, Wigan-based Smiths-Happiways also dabbled in stage carriage work. For the longer inter-urban routes, the five Duple Laser-bodied Tigers delivered in 1984 were retro-fitted with destination boxes and ticket machine stands, as being only 11 metres long and having fixed seats they were the vehicles least suited to tour work. Seen arriving in Derby bus station on the 201 service from Manchester is 303 (A155 XNE). (RS)

The higher of the two new Duple bodies was the luxurious Caribbean, and former Travellers of Hounslow KGS 486Y is seen outside Cleethorpes pier operating with John's Tours of Stowmarket. (RS)

A much-missed operator is Abbott's of Blackpool, whose red and grey coaches were a familiar sight across the North West. The introduction of the new Duple range saw it break two of its traditions, as with the purchase of MSU 611Y, the ex-Volvo B10M/Duple Laser demonstrator, it purchased its first non-British coach, as well as the first without its trademark number seven at the end of the registration. The next purchase returned to the norm, and Caribbean-bodied A547 HBV is seen parked outside Cleveleys depot. (RJ)

For several years the flagship of the coach fleet of Leon of Finningley was Van Hool Alizee-bodied Tiger 104, purchased new in 1983 as VKY 541Y. It was given the cherished number LEO 163 in 1989 and is seen leaving Doncaster South bus station on an excursion, the passengers obviously appreciating the photographer capturing them for posterity. (RS)

Yelloway switched from the Leopard to the Tiger as soon as it became available, taking twelve between 1981 and 1984. The majority were Plaxton Paramount 3500s for use on the flagship South West Clipper services between the North West and Devon. When Yelloway was taken over by ATL Holdings, the Tigers were quickly sold. South Yorkshire PTE purchased two for its Coachline fleet: 3910 WE (originally A578 KVU) and 3913 WE (originally A67 GBN). (RS)

West Riding was one of the four NBC operators to take the Alexander T-type, and here White Rose Express-liveried TE A33 LWX is seen loading in Barnsley bus station while working the X33 from Sheffield to Bradford. (RS)

Only twenty-three Tigers were bodied by Jonckheere compared to nearly three times as many by fellow Belgian Van Hool. West Yorkshire PTE purchased three Jonckheere Jubilee P50s shortly before the company was renamed Yorkshire Rider in readiness for privatisation. Originally registered B611 VWU, 1611 (GSU 340) is seen after repainting in National Express livery. (RS)

Before becoming the major player it is today, Robert Wright & Son was a small-scale manufacturer producing somewhat angular bodies primarily for the welfare market. It surprised everyone when it introduced the stylish Contour body in 1983. Complete with its swept back windscreen, rear wheels covered by spats and clever use of black to accentuate the sleekness of the body, it was unlike anything to have come out of the Ballymena factory. Ulsterbus was a major customer and took Contours for tour work and inter-urban services. One of the 11-metre inter-urban examples is seen here having passed to Reddin's of Muff. (MH)

In 1982, modifications including increasing the turbocharger pressure saw the TL11's bhp increased from 218 to 245. Van Hool-bodied Tiger 245 demonstrator A451 LCK is seen undertaking its duties in Brussels in 1984. (SG)

Two vehicles that could be described as slightly unusual are parked together at Llechwedd Slate Caverns. Leyland's unwillingness to offer a Gardner engine in the Tiger led Dennis to develop the Gardner-engined Dorchester in an attempt to win SBG orders. Faced with this, Leyland placated the SBG by offering the Gardner 6HLX from 1984. 403 BGO (originally B250 RNA) was one of the first two Gardner-engined Tigers delivered to a non-SBG operator, in this case A. Mayne & Son of Manchester. The coach to the left is one of the ex-East Kent AEC Reliances rebodied by Berkhof in 1984 and was operated by Knotty of Newcastle-under-Lyme. (MH)

Above and below: Talking of Berkhofs, between 1984 and 1986 London Country took delivery of fifty-three Berkhof Everest-bodied Tigers. The high bodies offered plenty of luggage space, making them ideal for airport services. As well as carrying a multitude of liveries, they had varying internal layouts ranging from standard fifty-three-seaters for National Express work to toilet-fitted thirty-seven-seaters with tables for use on the prestigious Speedlink services. BTL24 (B124 KPF above) was a fifty-three-seater liveried for use on Insight International tour work and is seen waiting its clients at Heathrow Airport, while BTL30 (C130 PPE), one of the luxurious thirty-seven seaters, is departing on the Speedlink service to Gatwick. (RC)

Willowbrook's final foray in bodybuilding was in offering budget-priced new bodies for rebodying older chassis. For bus work it produced the Warrior, a Leyland Lynx lookalike, and for coaching, the Crusader. Out of the fifteen built, only four were mounted on brand-new chassis: three on Bedford Venturers and a solitary Tiger, C744 JYA, was delivered to Safeway Services of South Petherton, Somerset. It is seen at Woburn Abbey shortly after delivery. (SG)

The Plaxton Paramount was built from 1983 until 1992, and while modifications were made over the years, the basic design remained unchanged. The Paramount II, launched for the 1985 season, incorporated minor visual changes, including the removal of the black grille moulding above the headlights. The body could now be specified without the small 'feature' side window, as shown by XIB 3916 (C769 KHL) parked at Blackpool Pleasure Beach coach park with examples of the Paramount's predecessor to the left and successor parked behind. (MH)

From the Paramount II, a low driving position option was also made available, with the driver sitting lower in the body so the passengers had a better view. The 3200 version used the two-piece 3500 windscreen, with the headlights mounted closer to the road. Seen in Weymouth in 1996, C233 HTX was owned by Dorset County Council Education Department but was new to Hill's of Tredegar. (RS)

The Paramount III featured bonded glazing and a moulded one-piece bumper, while the sloping side windows were replaced by a stepped waistline on both sides. Paramount 3500 E510 RFU was ordered by Peter Sheffield of Cleethorpes but entered service in 1988, just after the business had been acquired by Grimsby-Cleethorpes Transport. (RS)

Lowland Scottish was created in 1985 as part of the reorganisation of the SBG in preparation for deregulation and was the first of the former SBG companies to be privatised when it was sold to its employees in 1990. It took over the depots in the south-eastern corner of Scotland, and was one of the two SBG companies with depots in England. Indeed, Berwick-upon-Tweed is where we see Alexander TE-bodied D328 DKS, complete with its unusual roof-mounted mascot! (MH)

In 1986, Duple replaced the Caribbean and Laser with the 320 and 340, which, unlike their predecessors, shared a family resemblance, their model names indicating their height in centimetres. With its raked-back front, the Duple 340 was more striking than its low-height counterpart. Parked behind the Claremont Hotel on Eastbourne Seafront when brand new in 1986 is C213 NFV from the well-known black and green-liveried Blackburn-based fleet of Robinson's Holidays. (AS)

Belfast-based Ulsterbus, part of the government-owned Northern Ireland Transport Holding Company, is responsible for most of the bus services outside of Belfast. It also operates an extensive British mainland and continental European tour programme under the Ulsterbus Tours banner. New in 1986, Duple 340-bodied 5534 (JXI 534) is seen at Ryde Esplanade on an Isle of Wight tour in 1989 with vehicles from the Fountain Coaches subsidiary of Southern Vectis, the island's biggest operator, parked behind. (AS)

In 1987, following Eastern Scottish successfully trialling a prototype, the Tiger was offered with the Cummins L10 engine. Rated at 290 bhp, it was the most powerful coach chassis built in Britain, and to accommodate the L10, the chassis frame was revised with a wide centre section. The L10 was manufactured at Shotts in Scotland and was lighter than the TL11. In direct contrast to the vintage petrol pump is immaculate Duple 340-bodied G141 NPT, operated by Primrose of Acomb. (MH)

While the lower height Duple 320 was also an excellent choice for a touring coach, a number of operators chose it for inter-urban express operations, complete with destination boxes and vertically split entrance doors. South Wales operator Bebb of Llantwit Fardre took delivery of two such vehicles in 1989, both fitted with sixty-one seats. After sale by Bebb's, F59 YBO joined the fleet of Williamson's Motorways of Shrewsbury, where it was an ideal vehicle to operate Williamson's X96 service between Shrewsbury and Birmingham. (RS)

When is a Duple not a Duple? When it's a Plaxton. In 1989, declining sales resulted in the closure of Duple, with Plaxton purchasing the jigs for the 300 range. By 1990, Tiger sales had also slowed, and in an attempt to move stock, twenty-five chassis were fitted with the only Plaxton 321 bodies built, the 321 being Plaxton's reworked version of the Duple 320. Bebb's was the biggest operator of the 321, taking fifteen of the twenty-five. J25 UNY is seen at rest in Cardiff bus station while undertaking a National Express duty. (RS)

The Royal Tiger

The deregulation of the coach industry saw continental chassis manufacturers and bodybuilders making great inroads into the UK coach market, and while in most cases the vehicles were supplied in conventional body on chassis form, manufacturers such as Setra, MAN and Mercedes-Benz supplied integrally built vehicles. The three manufacturers mentioned had been slowly importing integral vehicles prior to deregulation, but with operators now looking to acquire coaches suitable for long-distance services running both in the UK and abroad, they became much more popular. No British manufacturer had anything to compete with these high-specification rear-engined coaches until 1982, when Leyland unveiled project B54, the Royal Tiger Doyen. Built of hollow rectangular section steel tubes with double thickness corner pillars, reinforced roof members and strong side pillars, the whole structure formed what was in effect a roll cage. It was powered by the same TL11 engine as used in the Tiger, but mounted at the rear, and this was available with Leyland's own six-speed manual, or five-speed hydracyclic fully or semi-automatic gearboxes. The interior of the body contained features never seen before in a British-built coach body: aircraft-style lockers rather than open luggage racks, the interior lighting had soft focus lenses and the light units were fitted flush with the roof. Outside, the Doyen body used clever ideas to make the body look even more startling, including a matt black surround underneath the windscreen, which heightened the effect of the already massive single piece of glass, while the headlights were the same as those used on Rolls-Royce cars. The three-piece Royal Tiger badge was (and probably still is) the most ornate badge to appear on the front of a coach.

The Royal Tiger was not intended to take orders away from the Tiger, but was aimed squarely at competing with the continentals. The Leyland empire contained a number of bus body building plants which were running under capacity due to the government phasing out the New Bus Grant and it was decided that production of the integrally built Doyen would take place at the Charles H. Roe plant at Cross Gates in Leeds. Unfortunately, production got off to a slow start due to a number of factors, one of which was the Roe workforce being more used to building batch production double-deckers rather than coaches built to individual orders. Leyland refused to allow Roe to improvise if errors were found in the design or specification plans, so any problems found in production caused delays though waiting for amendments to come from Lancashire, and as a result only ten Royal Tiger Doyens entered service in 1983. During the second half of 1983, Leyland decided to offer the Royal Tiger in chassis-only form and a set of sophisticated high-production jigs was installed at the Leyland plant at Workington in Cumbria. The initial plan was for Workington to produce the chassis-only version (which both Plaxton and Van Hool had expressed an interest in bodying), but soon afterwards production of the Doyen integral was also switched to Workington, with Roe taking responsibility for complicated special build orders. The Royal Tiger was the most advanced coach ever built by Leyland, and by 1986 improvements to the TL11 engine saw power output increased to 260 bhp, with the Cummins L10 engine and ZF gearbox also now available as options, but despite this the writing was on the wall. Production problems aside, manual gearbox versions had a propensity to go through clutches and the cable-operated gear selector linkages were problematic, resulting in an air-assisted system being retro-fitted at great expense to Leyland. By 1988 the last Royal Tigers had been delivered, and in its six-year life, ninety-eight Doyens, thirty-eight Plaxtons and twenty-eight Van Hools were delivered.

The third production Royal Tiger Doyen delivered was DAD 217Y, one of two delivered in July 1983 to National Travel West. A year later both moved to Wessex of Bristol, where they were part of the private hire fleet in what was a predominantly National Express-led operation. By 1990 it had received the registration USV 808 and passed to Jarvis of Maltby. (RS)

Even though it was registered after the coach above, Plaxton Paramount 3500-bodied WUV 417 (originally A382 NNK) was numerically the first production Royal Tiger to be bodied, entering service with Armchair Passenger Transport in December 1983. It too passed to Jarvis, both vehicles retaining their superb Royal Tiger badges – items which were prized by collectors and quite often 'went missing'. (RS)

Following privatisation, Devon General sold the Greenslades coaching unit to Nightingale's Coaches of Exmouth, which embarked on a fleet expansion programme that included A521 OCW, seen parked outside the MI5 building in Thorney Street, London. The coach was new to Mercer's of Longbridge who, despite being only 15 miles from Leyland, only ever ordered four new Leyland coaches. (AS)

Seen undertaking the driving trials at the 1984 British Coach Rally is Paramount-bodied Royal Tiger A138 RMJ from the fleet of Chambers of Stevenage. Whereas the Royal Tiger badge on the front of the Doyen was plastic encased, the Plaxton version was mounted on a wooden plinth, making it an even more attractive proposition for 'souvenir hunters'. (AS)

National London was the only one of the National Travel companies not to undertake regular National Express services, instead concentrating on incoming tourist work, private hires and holiday tours. National Holidays-liveried A656 EMY, the penultimate member of a batch of six Doyens, is seen turning into London Victoria in 1984. (AS)

The varied operations of National London are seen here with A653 SMY wearing Thomas Cook Holidays livery but loading in London Victoria in readiness for operating a National Express duplicate to Liverpool. (AS)

After withdrawing from the British Coachways consortium, Grey Green adopted the livery style but in its own colours, as seen on A839 SYR. Grey Green operated eight Royal Tigers, but this was the only Doyen, the rest all receiving Plaxton Paramount 3500 bodies. (AS)

Top Gear was the operating name of Pickup of Rochdale, which not only operated A717 GJA, one of the first Doyens to be delivered, but also took E317 OMG, one of the last two Royal Tigers to be registered. (AS)

National Travel (East) operated the largest Royal Tiger fleet, with eleven examples. The first six were intended to be Doyens but issues with delivery saw the whole order handed to Plaxton. A324 XHE is seen on the Brighton seafront while taking part in the 1984 British Coach Rally. (AS)

Sister ship A330 XHE was originally used on National Express Rapide services but is seen here in Bath bus station having passed to Crown Coaches of Bristol, where it was probably the most glamorous vehicle to have operated the Avon County Council-funded service 620. (RS)

With the privatisation of the NBC, West Riding's coaching arm Ridings Travel inherited part of the National Travel (East) fleet. A323 XHE is seen resting at Battersea coach park while working an excursion to the Ideal Home Exhibition. (AS)

Ridings Travel E48 TYG was delivered new to West Riding in 1988 and is seen in Wellington Street coach station, Leeds. The Paramount 3200-bodied Tiger in the background was operated by Northern Rose, formed when neighbouring NBC subsidiary West Yorkshire Road Car was privatised, while AEF 203Y, the Bova Europa to the right, was a member of the United Automobile fleet. (RS)

Originally registered A677 LBV, LHJ 736 had been new to Premier of Preston, a company under common ownership with Mercer's of Longridge. As with Mercer's, Premier's proximity to the Leyland factory didn't influence its buying policy and it was only the second new Leyland coach bought. Seen here in the ownership of Goodyear of Mapplewell, it had previously been used as a development vehicle for Bendix Brakes of Bristol and registered A567 UTC. (RS)

Van Hool was the only bodybuilder apart from Plaxton to build on the Royal Tiger underframe, bodying twenty-eight coaches. B348 AMH was one of eight similar vehicles new to Travellers of Hounslow but by 1989 it had passed to Maidstone Boro'line and is seen on a visit to Blackpool lights. (CE)

Van Hool-bodied Royal Tiger C171 AWK was originally registered HS 8882 and was new to Harry Shaw of Coventry. By 1990 it had passed to Leon of Finningley and is seen in the coach park at Bridlington. It was sold in 2002 to Kelly's Coaches, Enniskerry, Wicklow, Ireland, becoming 86 D 8471. (RS)

Turning into London Victoria is A419 FSA, one of a pair of Doyens delivered to Northern Scottish in 1984. Due to their primary use being on the Scotland–London services, they only seated forty-six. Hopefully the passengers were grateful for the extra leg room! (AS)

Please, no jokes about Scotsmen being careful with their money, but accident repair costs prompted Fife Scottish to come up with this 'alternative' front end arrangement using the front dome and flat screens from an Alexander AV body. New as A163 TGE, MSU 463 went on to become a mobile incident room with Fife Constabulary and is believed to now be a mobile home. (AS)

Two for the price of one. Travelling down Lakeside Way with Wembley Arena in the background are both of Crosville's Doyens. 429 UFM, leading, carries Euro Lynx livery, while 430 UFM, bringing up the rear, carries National Express livery. Euro Lynx was a short-lived continental holiday programme the coaches were bought for, and when it was discontinued the Doyens were moved onto the 545 National Express Rapide from North Wales to London. (AS)

The delivery of two Doyens to the newly privatised Badgerline in December 1986 coincided with its acquisition of Bath-based Roman City Coaches. Both were delivered in Roman City livery, as seen on 2401 (D401 GHT) at Wembley in 1989. They were both later demoted to local work, where their manual gearboxes and plug doors, which only opened when the handbrake was applied, did nothing to endear them to the drivers. (AS)

The last new coach delivered to Biggleswade operator Charles Cook was also a bit of a superstar, appearing not only on the Leyland stand at the 1985 Commercial Motor Show, but also on the cover of the Leyland calendar. Seen on Eastbourne's Marine Parade, C441 HHL was to stay with Charles Cook until operations ceased in 1998. (AS)

Pilgrim Coaches was formed in the run up to privatisation to take over the Southampton operations of Hants & Dorset's coaching arm Shamrock & Rambler. While the fleet consisted mainly of vehicles transferred from Shamrock & Rambler, six new coaches were purchased, including three Leyland-bodied Royal Tigers. C67 BFX was the first of the three and was the fifth Royal Tiger built by Leyland when production transferred to Workington. (AS)

Hailing from Fenton, one of the six towns making up the conurbation of Stoke-on-Trent, Procter's Coaches served the Potteries for over ninety years until operations ceased in 2012. C269 CRF is seen in one of the temporary coach parks set up to cater for the crowds attending Spalding Tulip Festival, an event which at its peak attracted over 100,000 visitors, most arriving by coach. (RS)

The other coach company in Rochdale was Ellen Smith, but unlike staunch AEC users Yelloway, it favoured its home county products. Two Royal Tiger Doyens were operated, both of which were used by Leyland for publicity purposes (indeed, D387 VAO retained its Leyland livery while with Ellen Smith). D892 PNB carried the registration D597 AJY while with Leyland and is seen departing Wembley at the end of the 1989 England–Belgium schoolboy international. (AS)

Paramount and Doyen in one. My former employer Potteries Motor Traction (or PMT as it was also known) made good use of its initials when it formed the ParaMounT Leisure coaching division. The fleet was a mix of Leyland Leopards, Tigers, Scanias and a solitary Royal Tiger Doyen, E42 JRF, which was also a visitor to Wembley for the schoolboy international. (AS)

After sale by Potteries, E42 JRF stayed local, joining the fleet of Bennett's of Cotes Heath, where until recently I would see it twice daily travelling through my village while undertaking my daughter's school run. It is seen here in Etruria on the outskirts of Hanley while on an evening jaunt for the Staffordshire Bus Enthusiasts' Club. (MH)

The last of the few. Sharing the honours with Pickup's E317 OMG as the last two Royal Tigers delivered, E785 BTV arrived with Nottingham City Transport in March 1988. It is seen here turning onto London's Buckingham Palace Road having just finished a National Express run from its home city. (AS)

A New Lease of Life

To finish off, ten Leopards that have been rebuilt and rebodied, showing that there's life in the old dog yet – or in this case, the old cat!

We start this chapter with a bit of a mongrel – not only was Horlock's of Northfleet's FHV 1 a rebody, but its new body was also second-hand. The Leopard chassis was new to Grey Green as SYX 573F and was fitted with a Duple Commander body. The body was originally fitted to JRK 621K, another Grey Green Leopard, which in 1983 was sent to Duple for fitting with a new Dominant body. Both chassis and body were deemed too good to scrap so they were mated together and fitted with a Supreme IV front end. The result is seen at Woburn Abbey in 1984. (TW)

CIÉ Tours was one of the biggest customers for the Van Hool Vistadome, taking forty-six in 1970/71, of which thirty-six were rebodied Leopards, including AZD 167, new in 1964 and originally fitted with CIÉ's own bodywork. The CIÉ Tours-liveried coach was seen working to Dublin Airport from Busaras, Dublin's central bus station. (MH)

This stubby-looking Plaxton Supreme was built on MCN 61, an ex-Northern General Harrington-bodied Leopard L2 from 1961. Barry Cooper from Stockton Heath near Warrington was by this time part of the Manchester-based Mayne Group. The somewhat grim picture was taken at Turner's coach park, just off Rigby Road in Blackpool. (MH)

Seen just after delivery to Grahams Coaches of Talke, Staffordshire, and still wearing the brown and cream livery of former operator Smith Aaron Coaches is Leopard HDG 368D. New in 1966 to Black & White Motorways and fitted with a Plaxton Panorama body, in 1979 it was fitted with a brand-new Plaxton Supreme IV body. Further improvements were implemented to bring it up to Graham's standards, including fitting a reconditioned engine prior to it entering service. (MH)

A unique vehicle was PWY 31W, rebuilt in 1981 by Independent of Horsforth using parts from Leopards CHA 114C and ex-Midland Red and ex-Ribble NCK 107J. The engine was moved to the rear and it was fitted with this modified Plaxton Supreme IV body. So great were the modifications that its chassis designation was changed from Leyland to Independent. It is seen here in 1984, shortly after purchase by Ivins Coaches of High Wycombe. (AS)

Another ex-Midland Red coach to receive a new body was WHA 252H, a 1970 Leopard that was fitted with a Duple Dominant III body in 1980. The work was done at the request of Barry Cooper Travel prior to its purchase by the Mayne Group. Sporting an original style Leopard badge and now registered OJP 908W, it is seen arriving at Wembley with a party of Widnes Rugby League supporters, ready to watch their team win the 1981 Rugby League Challenge Cup. (AS)

RHG 911X started life as RWR 977M, a Plaxton Panorama Elite-bodied Leopard new to Dearnway's of Goldthorpe. It is seen here with its new operator, Mercer's of Longridge, after being fitted with a new Duple Dominant IV body in 1981. (RJ)

Wearing National Holidays livery, ROG 550Y, from the Midland Red Coaches fleet, is seen departing Wellington Street coach station in Leeds en route to Bradford. The chassis was originally registered WHA 251H and was the sister vehicle to that seen on page 94. However, this time the Plaxton body has been replaced with an ECW B51 body. (RS)

As mentioned previously, the Willowbrook Spacecar was not known for its durability, and many of them were rebodied while still relatively young. In 1987, ten-year-old former National Travel East OKY 57R was sent to Duple, where it was fitted with a new 320 body for Eagre of Gainsborough. (RS)

Another Leopard receiving a Duple 320 body, this time the rarer 'express' door version, was former United Automobile Services Duple Dominant-bodied CUP 706S. The rebodying was done at the behest of Northumbria Motor Services, a company created from the northern section of United prior to privatisation. It is seen parked in Kirkbymoorside, now operating with Stephenson's of Easingwold. (MH)